Instagram Marketing

A Picture Perfect Way to Strike It Rich!

Mark Smith

Table of Contents

Introduction

Congratulations on downloading *Instagram Marketing: A Picture Perfect Way to Strike It Rich!* and thank you for doing so! We know that there are a lot of books out there about technology and social media, and we are really glad that you chose ours! In case you haven't noticed, technology is rapidly taking over the world. Chances are, more than half the people around you are on their cell phone or laptop at this moment. People no longer send mail by the postal service, rather they send a nice little text to a friend. Some people no longer buy clothes and shoes at malls, but rather on Amazon. The truth is that the smartest businesses have already taken notice of this and are plotting to maximize profit by using technology to sell their products. This book is going to teach you about marketing on one type of social media website that is increasingly popular - *Instagram.* If you take note of our tips, we bet that you will get your brand out there and increase your sales in no time!

First and foremost, the following chapters are going to share with you why technology is so important in today's world. They will introduce *Instagram,* a social networking app with more than seven hundred million users. From then on, you will learn the basics of creating a separate business account on Instagram and master the tricks that will help you interact with your potential new customers. You will know about the different communities on Instagram and learn how to direct your advertisements at people who will be the most responsive to your business.

Not only that, but you will also learn how to navigate the world of paid advertising and successfully blend in your ads with everyone else's normal posts. This book will show you how to do basic photo and video editing so that you can refine how your product looks in a picture.

Finally, we will show you how to use Instagram's "Insight" tools so that you will be able to see what type of person is attracted to your product or services and target towards that type of audience. We will show you how to use your location to communicate with locals near your small business, and we will make it a big success in your area when it comes to advertising!

There are so many books out there about using social media to your advantage, but thank you so much for choosing this book! We hope that you find this book both an enjoyable and useful read, and we bet that you will improve your business once you put our tips to practice!

Chapter 1: Why Instagram?

A Blast from the Past!

As you may have noticed, the world around us is constantly changing. Just the cell phone in itself has gone from a screen larger than your personal laptop to the small smartphones that we have today. Yeah, sure, it might not be *exactly* what Back to the Future predicted, but it's really not far off. Day by day, technology is vastly altering our lifestyle. We communicate with emojis, order Starbucks on our phone to skip the line and buy all of the season's newest trends online. People "scroll down the feed" to see pictures of elementary school friends, "like" our parents' Facebook statuses, and "share" the coolest memes with our internet friends. It is easy to forget that without the world of social media, we wouldn't have any of these conveniences.

Don't Know Much About History...

There have been prototypes of computers around since the 1940s, but nothing was fast enough to get anything done back then. Mainstream computers have been around since the 1960s, but there weren't many uses outside of conventional programming. In the 1990s, Tim Berners-Lee changed it all. He set off a new flame in the world of computers by inventing the World Wide Web, or what we know as "The Internet." Not long after, social media was born, with the first notable one, *Six Degrees,* debuting in 1996. Because of this, people began to share ideas and photographs with others who were halfway around the world and connect with long lost friends who were ten thousand miles away. The early 2000s saw the rise of *Myspace* and *AOL chat rooms,* and after *Facebook and Twitter* exploded in 2006, everyone was hooked onto some form of social media. Smartphones only fueled this fire, and suddenly, people far away from us in location were just a click away. Even though these social media websites were a huge success, a lot of them felt like a chapter book that was too long - there were only words and no pictures. Sure, there were profile pictures, but the main focus of a social media page was never on photos or videos. On October 6th, 2010, two friends in San Francisco, Mike Krieger and Kevin Systrom, changed the face of social media forever. that day at midnight, they launched their new app, *Instagram.* A combination of the words "instant camera" and "telegram," the new social media app *Instagram* allowed its users to share the most defining moments of their lives with their friends online. The app was a huge success. In just a month, two million people were using the app. Facebook acquired the app in 2012 and they are still constantly improving its functions. Today, one of their features even surpasses The use of *Snapchat.*

Now, What Does This Social Media Crap Have to Do with My Small Business?

The world of a businessman is fairly simple. You simply figure out where potential customers are and advertise your product or service there. As you can clearly see, people in developed first world countries probably use the Internet more than they leave their house. Ever since Instagram's launch, many businesses have begun to take notice of that, implementing the popular social media website into their marketing system. It's easy to use, and that has made it a clever advertising tool for so many different organizations! More than five million businesses worldwide, including *McDonald's* and *Lays Potato*

Chips, have hopped onto the Instagram bandwagon in order to increase interest in their products and find the right people to market to. With Instagram, many businesses do not even pay one single cent to get their products advertised if they know how to market the right way.

Shoot... How do I do this?

The business aspect of Instagram is very different from a personal account that you use to talk to your friends. The first thing you should do is sign up for an Instagram Business profile, separate from your other accounts. The good news is that although promoting advertisements requires a little bit of money, signing up for a so called "business" or "professional" account is completely free! Here is how you can sign up for an Instagram business account!

Step One: **Download the App!**

This really is only a good idea if you have a smartphone. The first step to starting your profile is having the means to do it in the first place! If you own an iPhone, head to the Apple Store, and if you own an Android, go to the Google Play Store to get the free app! Once it has finished installing, open the app!

Step Two: **Make Sure that You Have a Working Business Email Address**

It is easier to receive updates from the possible clients or partner businesses that you are following through email if you separate it from your personal one. Also, each account requires an email address that it is associated with. The good part about linking up a business email is that you can find all of your work contacts (co-workers, customers, and bosses that you keep in touch with) fairly easily through the "Find Friends" function on Instagram. Alternatively, you can provide Instagram with a phone number instead, if it is not already linked to another account that you have if you happen to have more people from work in your phone's contacts.

Step Three: **Open the App and Press *Sign Up***

 Use the email you just created or the new phone number that you have.

Step Four: **Enter the Right Contact Information (and Double Check if It's Correct)**

It's okay to enter your actual first and last name. You can switch to a Business Profile once you have your actual account created.

Step Five: **Pick a Profile Picture**

You HAVE to be strategic about this. There will be a +Photo button on the page. Click on it to add your picture. Make sure that this is a picture that you can recognize even from the small thumbnail, and be sure that it is relevant to your company. A good picture to use would probably be your company's logo if you have one, or maybe a mascot of your company. It's best to avoid your own personal picture because that represents you more than it represents the company.

Step Six: **Choose a Relevant Username**

This can be the name of your company, or it could be something that represents your company. You want to make sure that it is easy to find. When other people search your business on the search engine, you want them to be able to find your official business account.

Step Seven: **Link Your Facebook Account and Find People to Follow**

Instagram will want you to link your Facebook account so that you can connect with the people that you already know. Keep in mind that in order to switch any account to a business account, it requires a Facebook account as well, so be sure you link it to Facebook, either your business one or your personal one! Now, you can follow the Facebook friends that are affiliated with your business as well.

Step Eight: **Confirm Your Email!**

A lot of Instagram's functions are disabled if they do not know that your email actually belongs to you, so be sure to go to whatever email you linked it with and verify that it is your true email.

Step Nine: **Now that You Are Actually in the App with a Functioning Account, Change to a Business Profile!**

On the bottom of your screen, you will see a bar on the bottom with five icons. The first one is your home page. The second one is to search for more users, and the third one is to post. The fourth one lets you see your activity, while the last one with your profile picture on it lets you see your actual profile. Beside "Edit Profile," there is a small icon that looks like a wheel. Press that button and scroll down. Underneath "Blocked Users," you will see a button that says "Switch to Business Profile." Press that, and you are on your way to get started!

Step Ten: Enter Your Address When You Are Asked for it, and Your Business Email and Business Phone Number as Well

There will be a "Contact" button on your profile for those that want to ask you questions, and this is the easiest way to let them know how to reach you!

Step Eleven: Make Your First Post!

Now that you have all the basics set up, you are only one post away from starting an adventure of a lifetime! You will be able to cultivate and grow your business all on social media now. Make sure your first post introduces your business and entices potential customers! You could take a picture of your business building, a product that you feel like everyone would love, or even members of your crew!

Step Twelve: Share that First Post with Other Social Media Websites Like Facebook and Twitter!

Press the three dots beneath your picture comments once you have made your first post! You will find there that you will be able to connect your Instagram post with so many other popular social networking websites, increasing your potential fan base! Now that you have started posting, check the heart icon on the bottom bar in order to see who has liked your post, followed you, or even mentioned you!

Once you have the account, make sure you manage it daily and check your Direct Messages mailbox located on the top right corner just in case anyone wants to ask you any questions. You can let your close friends know about the account, and they can help attract more people to the page by following it. Congratulations!

Now that this is done, we are going to show you how to exploit the natural benefits that social media comes with. You do not have to pay Instagram in order to get new people to know about your business - you simply have to know how to find people who are interested and keep them enticed. The next chapter will make you and everyone else in your business the newest social butterfly on the block!

Chapter 2: YOU Are Instagram's Newest Social Butterfly: Ways to Connect with New Customers that You Never Would Have Thought About!

Now that you know all about the new world of Instagram and the basics of creating an account, it is time for you to learn how to make the most out of this app without spending a single cent. Paid advertisements are not the only way to succeed! You're probably wondering how you can successfully pick the right people to market to and rack in a lot of cash, so here are some foolproof ways that can help you increase your audience in seconds...

Make Sure Your Biography/Contact Information Is Correct

Before people will even look at all your posts, they will judge you by how you present yourself on your profile page. For business accounts, it is crucial that you have all your contact information right - that means name, address, phone number, and everything. If people try to contact you and cannot find you, they will get mad. In addition, be sure you have a convincing biography sentence that describes exactly what you do. It is a bonus if you can make it catchy as well. You need to explain what your brand or company offers and make it clear. Next up, have a link to your own personal website included. All of this can be changed with the "Edit Profile" button on your profile.

Finding Accounts with A Similar Niche/Common Interest And Interacting with Them

On your Instagram app, there is a bottom toolbar of five functions. Click on the magnifying glass, which is the second icon from the left. This is your "Explore" page. You can use the search engine to look for businesses similar to yours, go to their followers, and follow those people in order to gain attention. For example, if you are a daycare business, you can look up parenting clubs in your town and follow the people who are liking those posts. You will likely reach someone who is interested in your business or services. You can also message these people and send them special deals for your business through your Instagram Business account. The possibilities are endless, which brings me to my next topic. Once you find these people, it is easy to start a "Share for Share" campaign with a partner business.

Share for Share

Once you create your account and make posts, there are bound to be people who like your posts and/or comment on them. Reach out to those people and message them, asking them if they would like to share a post promoting your account in exchange for you doing the same for their business. Most of the time, underground businesses or businesses that have not gotten too big yet will agree to do this for you. This is like having an advertisement that is paid without actually paying for it. Your best bet is finding another account with a similar follower count (For example, if you are just starting out and have a hundred followers, find another account with a hundred followers as well). that will increase the chances of them saying yes to you. You can ask them to share your post through a comment on their page or a Direct Message (the mailbox on the top right corner of your Instagram app). Share for Share increases the publicity of your page and may even help you get a partner business.

Shout Outs

A shout out is a post thanking a customer for something they have done! If you see someone in your store buy a lot of your products and they do not mind being photographed in front of the store or being mentioned on Instagram, feel free to take a picture of them, upload it, and thank them for their business! Mention their name on the account! A lot of customers will appreciate that you actually took the time out of your busy schedule to get to know them and pay attention to them.

Kickstart Your Business With The Newest Trend: Hashtagging!

What are hashtags and why should I use them?
You may be asking what a hashtag is, or you may have already heard of it. After all, a couple did name their baby girl Hashtag in 2012. They were first used on Twitter, but they have moved over to Instagram as well. Hashtags are any word that follows a "#" sign (the hash or pound sign) that puts a post in a category. For instance, an ice cream shop owner might use the simple hashtag #food to get attention, and the CEO of American Eagle might make a newly branded hashtag like #AEO (American Eagle Outfitters) to represent their company. Hashtags can be put in the captions of Instagram posts so that people can search up posts in the category that they want to look at. According to a "Simply Measured" experiment and study, posts get 12.6% more activity when hashtags are used! There are strategic ways to use hashtags, and we are going to show you how to use them!

What are the different types of hashtags that I can use?

Brand Name (Branded) Hashtags

I know that most people would suggest that you pick a hashtag that is currently trending or popular, but brand name hashtags stick in your potential customers' heads and help them remember you. There are a few tips that will help you create a memorable hashtag. First, the suggestion is that you keep it short and to the point. You do not want to use any really complicated vocabulary words that will make your customers mistype your hashtag while posting anything themselves, so make sure that you use words that are both easy to remember and spell! Once you have decided on a hashtag name, you can use this on Instagram and many other social media web pages.

An example of a brand name hashtag is Coke's #ShareACoke campaign. Honestly, anyone who has been paying attention to the food community on Instagram probably knows about this hashtag since it is so simple and memorable. When Coke released the "Share A Coke" labels on all their bottles and cans, they created this hashtag so that friends could show each other online whenever they found a drink with the other person's name. Not long after, people started posting a lot of pictures of Cokes, thus helping the company advertise without spending any extra money! This hashtag is the perfect example of both a relevant and simple tag that many people can remember. Even today, many years after its release, people are still using this hashtag to post artsy Coke drinks on their profile. Just their posts may make you want to go grab a Coke now!

Brand name hashtags are good if you have a creative idea and want to keep a tagline that makes you stand out in the crowd, but like everything else, you always have the option of using another type of hashtag. You might want to consider creating another hashtag if you want to link it to a discount, contest, or another campaign.

Campaign and Contest Hashtags - Free Stuff and Free Publicity Attracts SO Many Customers!

You can also interact with your followers and get them to share your product on the internet by making a campaign hashtag. Campaigns or contests are often hosted by a small business or a big name brand in order to get attention. Prizes can vary - it can be a sample of your product, a cash prize, or maybe just the chance to be featured on your website provided that you have enough followers. This not only allows you to get your brand out there, but it creates a sense of community between all of your fans!

A good example of this type of hashtag is Ben and Jerry's "Capture Euphoria" campaign that they launched back in 2012. With hundreds of thousands of followers, the chain ice cream restaurant used #captureeuphoria to unite ice cream fans around the world. The idea is to take a unique picture with your ice cream (whether it be a selfie or one of someone else) and to upload it to Instagram and share your happiness eating ice cream with the rest of the world. By using that hashtag, the people who participated automatically got their picture uploaded onto a huge photo gallery website. The best ones got featured on the official Ben and Jerry's Instagram and local newspapers. The twenty best pictures got displayed on their professional advertisement! Though this contest did not have a monetary award, people who loved to get their picture featured participated - both buying an ice cream from their company and advertising online for all their friends to see! You simply have to come up with a contest and make a post, and your followers will do all the work for you!

Next, we'll discuss another type of hashtag that you may be more familiar with.

Trending Hashtags - Hashtags Dependent on Special Occasions, the Season or Date, and Etc.

Trending hashtags are simple. They are simply hashtags popular for a specific day! For instance, if you were selling American flag print bikinis for the Fourth of July, you could try to promote your post with the hashtag #4thOfJuly a week before the holiday. A popular example of this is #SelfieSunday. On the internet, many teenagers and adults alike love to post a selfie of themselves on a Sunday using this hashtag. If you are a clothing business, you can use this to your advantage by including it in your caption so those people that like to look at different people's Sunday selfies can find you as well. It is not a good idea to only use these hashtags because often, many people are using them and it will be hard to find your post even ten minutes after you post it. However, it isn't much extra work to maybe add just one of these on to the end of your caption. Who knows, even one extra person viewing your post is still extra publicity for you.

Common, Everyday Hashtags and Their Uses

There are also hashtags that everyone else uses. These are the hashtags that are not exclusive to businesses, such as #coffee or #yoga. Though these hash tags may not gain you much publicity because of a number of people looking at it, it may still reach a few people. However, as a business, you must know that people craving the type of product you sell may be looking at these hashtags to see what choices they have. For instance, if you are a local coffee shop, you can take a picture of your famous mocha and use #mocha to attract more coffee drinkers.

This Is Especially Important for Small Businesses - Use Geographical Hashtags to Your Advantage!

Even if you live in a place, you still may not know about every little business in the area. Luckily, by hashtagging whatever place or city your business is in, customers have a greater chance of finding your shop when they need your particular service. For instance, if you live in New York City and have a computer shop there, you can use #NYC and make a post about your services so that locals know where you are in the middle of a busy, crowded city. The minute locals know about your business and fall in love with your services, they will gossip to their friends and spread your name out there in your community. The money comes rolling in.

So How Do I Find Popular Hashtags to Use?

Use the "Explore" page on your Instagram (second item on bottom toolbar" to research posts similar to yours. This whole page generates posts for you to look at based on the people that you follow, the posts that you like, and the people that interact with you on Instagram. Here, you can find the hashtags that businesses around you are using and the hashtags that people selling similar products are using. The truth is, researching what hashtags your competitors are using will not only help you figure out how many hashtags to use and which ones, but it also provides a chance for you to look at someone else's product and figure out how yours can be better.

How Do I See if My Hashtag Is Doing Well?

When someone posts a caption with a hashtag, the hashtag always appears in blue font rather than a black font. This is because it is a link. Once you click on the hash tagged word, you can see every post that involves that hashtag! This is very useful if you are tracking a hashtag you created specifically for your brand or a contest.

How Many Hashtags can I Use?

You can use as many as you want! Many people will use around one to five to avoid "spamming" with a hashtag.

Hashtags are a way to increase visibility and attract people with a common interest to your business, all at no cost at all!

Mentioning, Tagging, and Direct Messaging (Otherwise Known as DMing): Let Your Fans and Partners Know that You Are Noticing Them!

Now that we are on the topic of captions (with hash tagging), it is also worth noting that "mentioning" or "tagging" your followers on your posts can increase your visibility and make you more approachable as a business.

While posting a picture, there is an option called "Tag People." Here, you are returned back to your picture and you can press on a face or an object to tag another account, thus letting them know that you have posted. You can tag people in photos and tag loyal customers in a post about a product. The choice is yours, but this tool allows you to show everyone else the people related to your post.

Mentioning is also another choice that you can make as an Instagram marketer. While writing a caption or commenting on either your own post or someone else's post, you can press the "@" key and follow it up with someone's username to mention them. This can allow you to notify other people that you are needing to say something to them!

Finally, there is a small icon near the top right corner of your screen called the "Direct Message" icon. You can use this function to privately message anyone of your choice. You can use this to discuss business with partner companies or to answer questions that loyal customers or new people have.

Instagram Live: It's Like TV, But It's Just for Your Business

How would you like it if people could look at what your business is doing at a specific set time, or if your business could have its own little show just like *The Bachelorette* or *Grey's Anatomy?* This is all made possible with a 2016 addition to Instagram called Instagram Live. By swiping left and then switching to the "live" option, you can create and stream a video with all your followers. Instagram will notify all of your followers that you are going live. While you are streaming, the people who are watching your video can comment their opinions or questions and like what you are doing. Now you're probably wondering why you need to go live to advertise your business. For one, it increases your visibility/publicity and makes your business stand out against competitors. You can also get more up close and personal with those that follow you. There are plenty of things you can do with the Instagram Live feature!

Here are some things that you should probably do before you start an Instagram Live video:

- Know the information about your company. If someone asks you a question, you want to be able to answer it fully. If you have a knowledgeable employee at your business, they can take over this job as well. Know your products inside and out!

- Dress more professionally so people take you seriously.
- Advertise before the session! Make posts or promote the session to people you know who live around you. You don't want to start a live session, reserve that time out, and then have nobody show up.
- If it is a tutorial on how to do something or a tour around your business, practice! Treat this as if you were giving a public speech to thousands of people because that is basically what you are doing (except over the Internet). Remember that you are your business' representative when you are going live!

Now, here are some ways to take advantage of the tool...

Start Question and Answer Sessions and Ask Customers What They Want

The magic of Instagram Live is that it allows you to connect with your fans or followers on a face to face basis. This means that you do not have to go through all the nonsense of emailing, texting, calling, or sending people videos and pictures just to answer one question. They can comment the question on your live session, and you can answer them right then and there. Now they are not the only ones to know the answer to that question, but other people can also benefit from their question as well. Customers will often leave you a "heart," which represents a like, whenever their question is answered. Before the Question and Answer session, you can make a post letting your customers and partner businesses know about the time and date that you will be doing it on. Instagram Live (unlike Snapchat stories or Instagram stories) do not have a minimum or maximum time limit put on it. This means that the session can last as long as you want it to. On top of it, there is a record of every person who watched your video. This way you know who is really interested in your business and/or the products that you are selling. This can help you better figure out what kind of person to advertise to and keep track of loyal customers.

How-To Sessions and Other Tutorials for Cooking Businesses, Tutoring Businesses, Sports Coaches, Music Teachers, etc - Capturing Your Work in Action!

This one is mainly for people that are offering services rather than a product. Often times, before people choose one person that offers a service, they shop around first to see who is the best at what they are offering. Show your customers what you've got! Make them fall so in love with the way you do things that they throw cash at your door so that you can teach them how to do things.

For example, if you coach club soccer, you can stream a video of practice and let all the mothers watch how you teach children before they decide to enroll in your program for the year. If you are a makeup artist at Sephora, you can film a customer (with their permission) and show everyone else what you can do. If you do a good job, girls will be flocking at your door to do makeup for their wedding, prom, or other special occasions. If you own a cooking business and would like to host a special video to show customers how to make one specific item, you can Livestream your cooking process. If you have a teaching or tutoring job, you could stream a video of you teaching a class so that people can see your style and figure out for themselves if they like the way you teach. This gives people a personal feel to your services even if they are not there with you.

In order to do this, you would need something to hold your phone in place, like a phone stand or a small tripod. However, there are many benefits to this even though you do probably have to buy a tripod. People know what exactly they are getting into, so they are more inclined to pick you over someone else they know nothing about!

Introduce a New Product Through Instagram Live!

Customers do not always notice new products, even if you put them in the store. However, most people do check the internet every single day. With Instagram Live notifying every follower that you are now online, it is so easy to tell people all the details about a product that they might have otherwise never known about. The comment function will allow interested people to ask anything they want to about your product, and you can present it in the best light possible! This may also get people in the community talking about your product, and it is no less effective than any commercial that you see on TV! You can even give your phone number and let them buy the product right then and there from you, or you can link it to an online website that will allow them to place orders. that is if you are able to ship packages to their house. If not, they can always pick it up in store. If you're selling toys, go ahead and show people all its new features! If you're selling makeup, find a model and apply that lipstick on her! Once people see the product in use, they will be more than head over heels for it!

Discounts, Discounts, Discounts! How You Can Use People's Love for Cheap Stuff And Turn It into Profit!

Spend fifty dollars in a store and get ten dollars off! Who buys a whole bunch of stuff they are probably never even going to use when there is a coupon involved? Let's face it, everyone does! With Instagram Live, you can occasionally offer your customers a coupon code that they can only get when they watch your live story. When people hear about this (and don't know when the next coupon code will be given), they will watch your story every time that you go live! This gives you the opportunity to attract more viewers on your story, thus increasing your publicity.

"It's The Hard Knock Life for Us" - Show Your Customers Your Everyday Job - Make Your Business More Approachable!

Do you ever wonder about what a business does behind the scenes? Customers never really stop wondering about the process it takes for their products to be made. This is why you can use this to attract them to your Instagram story! It is always interesting to get to know the people that run a business! This is like a meet and greet at a concert - make your business look fun and approachable, and let people figure out what you do daily! When you do this, customers are more likely to see you as a friendly business than a place that is just out to get their money. This is a very humbling experience, and you do not even have to worry about your information leaking out because this is live and not recorded at all! Who knows, people may like the way you run your business so much that they want to become your future employee! You really never know.

Remember that Instagram Live increases your visibility and publicity. With so many people knowing about your business, your profits are bound to go up if you just know how to use this correctly! Of course, however, if you prefer for an announcement to be out for more than just one hour of live streaming, you may want to consider Instagram Stories instead.

Instagram Stories: A Twenty-Four Hour Advertisement

What if you wanted to post something on your feed but didn't feel like it was important enough? Instagram recognized this problem, so they created a function called the Instagram Stories. This feature was added to Instagram back in 2016. This makes Instagram similar to a competitor social media app, Snapchat. If there is something that you would like to share, but you do not feel like it is notable enough to be a post in itself, a story post is your perfect option.

How It Works

The videos you post can be up to fifteen seconds long, but they can be shorter if you want them to be. You can post as many photos or videos as you want. Whatever you post is up for twenty-four hours. If you don't feel like the raw video or photo is interesting enough, you can add filters and stickers on it, as well as text, emojis, or things you draw. Whatever you post will be at the top bar of everyone else's Instagram app, and they can view it if they want to or choose to ignore it if they do not want to. Even in the first six months of Instagram Stories' release, one hundred and fifty million people had already used it. It has been growing in popularity, perhaps even surpassing Snapchat's beginning stages.

How Can I Post a Story?

Here is how you post an Instagram story. Go to Instagram and swipe right once you get to your home page. Here, you will access the Instagram stories camera. You can post a normal picture of a product to advertise it, or you can go to "Boomerang" and it will post your picture in small snippets with a staggered effect if you want a dramatic look. There is also a rewind button if you want to play a video backward for fun, and a hands-free video recording option. Once you are done, you can press next and send it to your story, and ta-da, it is done. You can also turn the flash off if you are taking a picture of technology or in the bright daylight. Even if you don't like the post, you can press the X button and start all over.

- Filters: You can swipe right after you have taken the picture to add a filter. These often polish up your picture and if it is a picture of your employees, they would probably appreciate it!
- Art and Drawing Options: In order to draw on your picture or add some sort of comment with your own handwriting, you can click on the icon that looks like a pen on the top right corner of the page. Once you are there, you can select any color and decide on what you want.
- Adding Fonts or Text: Press the Aa button, then you can add a little mini caption right on your picture! You can move it around the picture as well.
- Stickers: There are so many Instagram stickers for you to choose from! There are more than just the traditional emojis at your disposal. There are

random stickers about your location, the time, and more.

- In the future, you will be able to add a LINK to the picture on your story! For now, that is still in beta testing and only available to specific accounts.

Instagram stories can be used for the same things that the Live stories can be used for. It may be easier to start promotions or coupons through the stories since it is there for twenty-four hours.

Now you know a lot of the basics you need to interact with your customers online. With the right people managing your Instagram account, you can appear as an approachable and friendly business and promote whatever new products, services, or deals that you have going on right now. However, even with all the amazing benefits of natural marketing online, sometimes you still need paid advertisements to get your business out in the first place. The next chapter will show you how to navigate the world of Instagram's paid advertisements, tell you about how much they cost, show you their benefits, and reveal the different types of advertisements that you can create.

Chapter 3: Paid Advertisements: When a Little Cash Spent Turns into a Lot of Cash in Your Pocket

Instagram offers a whole new world of advertising through its paid options. The good news about paid advertisements is that every single ad blends right in with the rest of the person's visible "news feed," making it hard to ignore when it seems like a regular post. In addition, Instagram is pretty smart. Once you pay for an ad, it makes sure that your ads are reaching your "target audience," or the types of people that you want it to reach (to maximize the profit of your business, of course!).

There is nothing that you want to spend money on more than an Instagram ad. People rarely read newspapers or magazines anymore, and many people go on the Internet to shop for whatever they need. This makes it easy to advertise on social media, which is still often cheaper than actual advertisements in the paper. The truth is that if you want to spend money on any social media website, it is best for you to spend it on Instagram. Research has shown that it has the most active community, surpassing both Facebook and Twitter.

However, you have to remember that Facebook bought Instagram about five years ago, so every Instagram ad has to run through Facebook's Ad Manager. Luckily for you, Facebook Ad Manager is a very simple process, and it takes only about a few minutes to start up an ad.

There are so many different types of advertisements that I am going to introduce you to before I show you how to activate them!

1) Photo Ads: These advertisements are promoted with both a description and any sort of artsy/edited or natural picture of your choice. These are the most basic types of advertisements, and you can create one through any photo editing app or camera app there is.

2) Video Ads: You can create up to a sixty-second video to display as an advertisement. It will blend in with all of the other posts (that they follow) that the person sees. These videos can also be accompanied by sound, so you can describe a product in full or ask your followers for advice on how to improve your company.

3) Carousel Ads: Is one picture not enough for you to describe your company's goals and objectives or to promote your current deal? Create a carousel ad to where you can post up to ten pictures in one post! This way, you can promote various products or show different aspects of your company! It is better to pick the Carousel Ad anyway just because it allows you to post multiple pictures. This helps you get the biggest deal out of what you pay for!

4) Story Ads: These are very similar to Snapchat's stories. When browsing through your friends' stories, you may sometimes see a "Sponsored" story that seems to appear out of nowhere. These are paid story advertisements, and you can create one for your business too. This way, everyone gets to see your advertisement before they get to see their friend's story.

How to Create an Instagram Ad

First of all, you need to create a Facebook Page. This can be done through your personal Facebook account, and this page will be linked to your Instagram business account. It is hard to give you a definite price that your ad will cost because it depends on the end goals of your ad and who you want to target it to.

There are two mainstream ways that people mainly use to start creating ads on Instagram.

- The Ads Manager (on Facebook). This is a step by step guide through Facebook that helps you create an ad. For one, it will ask you about your "marketing objective." You can decide if you want to spread the name of your brand around or simply let the ad "reach" new people that have not seen it before. Next up, you will need to decide the main goal of this ad and beyond that. Do you want people to go to a different link, not on Instagram (like a website to buy things)? In that case, select the Traffic ad. You can also target the ad to where you will get more people talking about the product through comments, likes, and shares. that's called Engagement, so if you want that, select the Engagement ad. There are many more options, but once you have selected yours, it is time to start on your ad! They will ask you for some information, including where you live, the money you use, and the time zone that you are in. This is so that they can better tailor your ads to the right audience. Speaking of your audience, the next step you take is selecting your audience. You can target the location, ages, and gender that you want to see your ad. You can also choose to only tailor the ad to people who speak English if all you speak is English. Perhaps the most useful tool for this Ads Manager is the "Detailed Targeting" function. Here, you can tailor the ad to anyone with a specific interest. For example, McDonald's would tailor their ads to "fast food lovers" or "french fry lovers." You can also send the ad to people who like a specific another page. This gives you the edge over your competitors because if you're another local coffee shop, you can promote your ad to everyone else in the area who liked Starbucks' Instagram profile. The important part comes next. You have to set your budget now. For instance, you can set a daily budget of ten dollars so that your company will never spend more than ten dollars a day on an advertisement. This helps you save money and get your business out there at the same time by finding the most efficient way to start a business. After this, you connect both your Instagram account and your Facebook page, and then you are done! Your ad is up and running, and people will start finding your business in no time!

- The Power Editor: This option is also on Facebook, and it is also fairly easy to use. Once you get to the Power Editor, press "Create Campaign." You enter in your information, and it basically takes you back to the Ads Manager. You then enter in all your information and budget, just like you would in the regular Ads Manager. Most people only use the Power Editor to manage several different ads at once.

Tips to Make the Most Out of Different Types of Advertisements

1) For photo ads, make sure that you are keeping it simple and to the point. In a picture, there is not much room to express your message, so less is more. Add stickers, writing, and text, but do not make it so big and distracting that it takes away from your product.

2) Put a link on your advertisement, and link it straight to your online website that your company may have. Go to your ad and press "Promote," and pay to put the website link on the ad. This allows people to go straight to that page to buy your product if they like it.

3) Use carousel ads to tell a story. Keep it interesting. No one wants to hear about a cleaning tool and what it looks like, but if you tell a story about how a single mom of three kids used that to simplify her busy schedule, all of the sudden, people sympathize with her and pay more attention to your product.

4) People will scroll past your ad if it is a blatant ad, similar to how we all hang up on a call that is blatantly selling something. Integrate your ad into people's Instagram feeds and make it blend in.

5) Keep your ads consistent and make them look similar. It helps add to your brand name if people can spot a picture and know it is from your company.

6) Use Instagram Video. Not many people have the time and patience to create a video. that makes videos stand out from thousands of pictures that people scroll past every single day. Videos are also useful - if you are going to spend money on an ad, you might as well show your customers what your product can do. Put that electric bike to the test and capture a bunch of models having fun in your brand's bikini. When people see that other

people are having a good time with your product, they are way more inclined to buy it!

7) Add A Call To Action! - Call To Action is a simple trick that you can add to your advertisement that makes the customers able to press one button and go straight to a website or an app downloading page. You don't have to tell people to go to the link in your biography for a promotion. Set up a call to action and one simple button will take them to a link!

8) Use Hashtags! You need to use hashtags in advertisements too, not just regular posts. This way, people are reminded of your brand name's hashtag or can find you through a common hashtag. It never hurts to include one!

Chapter 4: Photo and Video Magic! How to Sell Your Product Just Through the Superpower of Editing

Let's face it. Just like no one likes looking at an ugly stripper, no one likes looking at an advertisement that is bland and not unique at all. Part of selling your product is packaging it right; part of having an ad succeed on Instagram is making it right. This is why photo and video editing becomes so important in today's technological age. If it doesn't look good, many customers will not even give your product a chance before they condemn it to hell. This chapter will show you the basics of video and photo editing through a few free and popular apps, helping you make your product look as neat as possible. Once you know how to sell your product, people will constantly be signing up to get it.

There are many apps out there that can help you edit a photo. Of course, you don't want to edit it to the point where people do not recognize the model wearing your clothing or your product in itself. However, the right edits can make your products look higher class.

We'll start with VSCO, the most popular photo editing app in the Instagram community. This app is available through both the Apple Store and Google Play Market. The best part about it is that it is completely free for you to use! Though some may see this app as a photo blog only, it has many photo editing options that can help your product or service have the professional look to it. You do not even need to touch the blog part of it at all. When you first open the app, sign up for an account to access all the tools. Then, a screen with a plus sign should pop up. Press the plus sign to import your photo, and you can edit it from there. Once your photo is uploaded, select it and then press the button with two lines on the bottom left-hand corner. This starts your editing process.

- FILTERS: These are especially useful if you are promoting a fashion business (such as modeling) or a travel business that requires you to take scenic pictures of the world. When you first load up the picture in the editor, this is the first function that it will take you to. You should select one that works, then click on it. You then get to pick the intensity of the picture. The left circles mean that the filter is weaker, and the right circles show that the filter is stronger. Take your pick. There is a free set available on VSCO, but you have to pay if you want the others.
- BRIGHTNESS AND CONTRAST: Press the button with two lines again, and click on Contrast. This will allow you to change how light some parts of the picture are and vice versa. You want to increase this if you want your center product to stand out from its background.
- EXPOSURE: This one is basically adding a white light/sunlight to a picture. This might be needed if you are taking a picture of the sunny beach and would like a more dramatic effect.When you're done, press the check mark and go to the next function.
- STRAIGHTEN: You can adjust the picture if you took it at a slightly altered angle, you can get it fixed right away. that way, your product is at the

center, and there will be nothing to distract the viewer from it! Simply move the bar from left to right to straighten your picture.

- HORIZONTAL/VERTICAL PERSPECTIVE: This is similar to the straightening tool. It focuses on the angle you took the picture at.
- CROP: This is oh so important for photo advertisements! You can use this to crop photos to Instagram size. Though Instagram tends to take advertisements of many different crops, it is best to use the traditional one to one dimension!
- CLARITY, SHARPEN, and SATURATION TOOLS: These all help add color and make your ad clearer than it could have been.
- VIGNETTE: These will help add drama to your travel photos if you are in that business, or perhaps a picture of a fancy restaurant or modeling service as well. Use this to your advantage because it adds a tiny dark border to the picture. This causes you to focus on the center object.

The rest of the VSCO tools are not really that relevant to photo advertisement editing, but keep these tools in mind and you are probably set. You do not want to edit the photo so much that it looks completely fake and like the opposite of what you are selling, but these tools can help enhance your product just enough to where someone who was just thinking about purchasing your product or service might just go ahead and buy it.

There is also another app that you can use. Although it costs around four dollars, this app allows you to edit your pictures and place text on it as well. The good news is that it goes ahead and places the text for you in an artsy manner, and you do not have to spend much time editing the photo. This app is called "Over," and it is available for both Android and the iPhone. This is mainly a typography or text editor app, but it may come in handy if you are trying to design a paid advertisement.

If you prefer a simple app that concentrates more on brightness and contrast, you may prefer an app called Afterlight. This is available on iOS, Android, and Windows. This app allows you to change the color, saturation, and angle of the picture really well. It only costs ninety-nine cents.

Having a Consistent Style on Instagram for Your Business

Though it is fun to experiment with various different filters and different fonts, it can get a bit inconsistent if you are trying to build up the name of a brand. People will find your posts hard to recognize in a crowd, and they will not be as memorable if you just edit whatever you want. To have a certain signature look, you have to design your Instagram feed like you would design a room in your house. Everything should look neat and have a certain style to it. The good news is that you get to pick your style!

First of all, you should decide on a specific "tone" or "feeling" of the whole page. Do you want it to be lighthearted or darker? This really should depend on the type of product you sell. For instance, if you are a makeup and beauty product store, you probably should not have a page that gives off an eerie vibe like a haunted house.

Next, you need to decide on a few signature filters that you will use for your business. This doesn't mean that you need to choose just one, but it is probably best if every single one of your posts is polished with one out of five filters to keep it simple and memorable. If you want to, you could also ditch the filter altogether and go with a natural look of the photo.

With text, you could create a company watermark if you would like. If that is way too much trouble for you, you could consider keeping all your fonts on posts the same two or three signature fonts so that your posts still maintain a unique look.

Finally, you should decide on a color scheme. Ideally, it should be your company's colors, but try to keep this consistent. This way, if anyone sees those few colors put together, they are automatically reminded of your particular product and company. The idea is not to have so much fun with editing that you do not keep a recognizable style!

Adobe Photoshop Basics

Sometimes, a phone editor is simply not enough, and you want to create a more artsy ad for a special product or event. Adobe Photoshop is the premier program for photo editing if you want to create the prettiest ads. The downside is that the program is expensive, but if your business can afford it, this is a really good tool for creating advertisements. The program has a thirty-day free trial if you are only interested in making a few official advertisement pictures and never want to touch the program again after that!

Here is how you use some of the basics located on the toolbar of Adobe Photoshop.

- MOVE TOOL (Press V on the Keyboard to activate it) - This tool looks like a compass and a little triangle. Click on it and you can drag anything on your screen and move it to another place.

- CROP TOOL (Press C on the Keyboard to activate it) - This icon looks like a square with edges not cut off with a slash right through it. You should just enter the dimensions you want once you press on this tool, and it will give it to you. This is helpful for making all your business advertisements perfect for Instagram and the right size!

- THE MAGIC WAND (Press W on the Keyboard to activate it) - This icon looks exactly like a wand. This removes anything around a spot with a similar color. This is helpful if you want to replace a color with another one or change the background on an image.

- CLONE STAMPS (Press S on the Keyboard to activate it!) - This looks exactly like it sounds. It is a stamp icon. This is what you can do to cut someone out of a picture (like a photobomber who interferes with a picture of your product). It takes the background around it and makes one area of the picture blend right in with the background.

- PAINTBRUSH AND THE PENCIL OPTION (Press B on the Keyboard to activate it!) - Th

- ERASER (Press E on the Keyboard to activate it!) - This is pretty self-explanatory. You move your mouse over whatever you want to get rid of and it's gone.

- PAINT CAN (Press G on the Keyboard to activate it!) - This icon looks exactly like a spilled can of paint. You can use this to fill in backgrounds with either a solid color or a gradient (like going from white to green or going from blue to purple, etc).

- TYPE TOOL (Press T on the Keyboard to activate it!) - For business people like you, this may be the most important tool that you can use on an advertisement.

This tool looks like a giant T on the toolbar. You can select whatever font you want, whatever size you want, and rotate it however you please. This is really useful if you want to put the name of your business, product, or the promotion onto your picture itself instead of putting it in a caption that people might not even read.

- SHAPE TOOL (Press U on the Keyboard to activate it!) - This lets you create geometric shapes to design your ad with. It looks like a rectangle on the toolbar.
- LASSO TOOL (Press L on the Keyboard to activate it!) - This icon looks like a small paper origami bird trying to fly up. The lasso lets you "mask," or select an oddly shaped item and drag it out of the picture by simply selecting around its corners. This one is harder to use but very rewarding if you know how to use it the right way.
- HAND TOOL (Press H on the Keyboard to activate it!) - It's sad to say that something this simple might be the most useful tool in all of the Photoshop. It is shaped exactly like it sounds - it looks like a giant Mickey Mouse hand. You can use this tool to go back to anything you did and drag it out of the picture if you do not like where it is placed. You can move things around with this.
- ZOOM TOOL (Press Z on the Keyboard to activate it!) - The zoom tool looks like a magnifying glass. It lets you view the small things in the middle. You can use this to edit the finest details of a picture.

There are many other tools on Photoshop and it takes years to master, but if you know these tools you should be set on making a simple advertisement.

Finally, there is one more trick to working with Instagram. Now that pictures can zoom, a picture of your product can look really cool if you have to zoom in to see what it really looks like. This is different from how many people post and elicits attention if you know how to do it right.

Now that you know how to make your advertisements pretty and packaged, you need to know when exactly you need to post your pictures that you worked so hard to edit!

Chapter 5: Timing, Location, and Demographics! Target the Right People and You're Set

When should I post? Will the people around me know that I posted? When are people actually looking at their social media apps? Am I just being annoying and posting way too much? These are all questions that need to be answered in order to know when exactly to post to make the most out of your marketing/campaigning.

First of all, you need to know how to track how well your posts have been doing. Once you open up Instagram, press the fifth button (the furthest one to the right) on the bottom toolbar. This leads you to your profile. You will need to click on that then look at the top toolbar where your username is. Beside your username, there should be a few bars (an icon that looks like a bar graph). Press that. This is your "Instagram Insights" button, and it will tell you a lot of information about your followers and engagement. It will show you how well your posts and stories are doing, and what kind of person (gender, age, location) most prefers them. This will help you decide who to target your advertising and products towards next time. You will get to see your impressions, which is the number of people that have viewed your posts, even if they have done nothing.

Honestly though, it is not enough to know only the demographics of your followers. You might not know this, but you can also use your own geographic location to boost sales and gain publicity on Instagram.

The World of Geotagging

Every phone has a tracker in it. No, it's not some ploy by the government. Rather, it is a GPS chip that helps you navigate the world you live in. Because of this, "geo tagging" your posts on Instagram is easy. Geotagging is basically the fancy term used for sharing your location with someone (your latitude and longitude coordinates on a map). Don't worry about accidentally leaking your location, because Instagram will not share it with your post unless you instruct it to.

So how exactly do you add a geotag to a post? Believe it or not, it is actually fairly simple. When you upload a photo, you can instantly press "Add Location" on there and select a city or a place. Your location will appear as text underneath your username on your actual post.

This comes in convenient because you can click on that location and instantly be directed to all the different posts that have ever been taken before at that location! It is an excellent tool.

Not to mention, you can list your business as one of the location tags. When pressing "Add Location," just select the custom location button and add your store to the Instagram database. This way, everyone who has ever been at your store can tag the pictures of themselves in your store or the picture of all the products they get and share it with their followers! Any frequent customer who clicks the business location geotag might be able to see your newest products and sales, and anybody who does not know anything about your business will now know what you offer! If you have a special event and customers geotag it, they may attract new customers who show up at your front door!

Creating a geotag is the first thing you can do for your business if you want your customers to start posting about the products that they get.

How Often Do I Post, and When Should I Post to Reach the Most People?

You want to post just enough for people to remember that you exist, and you want to not post so much that you scare off all your potential customers because they think you are spamming.

If you post a picture of your newest product at two in the morning, you're not likely to get many views, likes, or comments in the few hours after you post it. Like a game of chess, posting things on Instagram requires strategy, and timing is one of those things you want to get right if you do not want to waste your time posting things that no one will see.

Unlike Facebook, Twitter, or even your own email, most people check Instagram many times a day. This app is easy to check throughout the day because a picture feed is easier to scroll through than one with a whole bunch of words. Nevertheless, there are still peak times.

According to a study conducted by SumAll, you should post around five to six in the afternoon on Mondays through Fridays. This is when people normally get off work and go grab a bite to eat, so they often have time to grab out their phone and scroll past their Instagram feed.

Even with that information, it is good to remember that it is important for you to look at your posts and see when your own followers and community get on Instagram. When you go to the "Instagram Insights" button, you can see when people are commenting on and liking your posts. You may want to cater to your own clientele once you have an established community who supports your small business.

Another thing that you should remember with posting is consistency. No one wants to follow a business account that does not post very often, no matter how good your business is. No one will remember your account if you only post once a month. In fact, according to blogs on Bufferapp, Union Metrics noted that the businesses who posted around one or two times a day attracted the most audience on their posts and had the most people interacting with them.

Does Posting Pictures of People Increase My Engagement?

Yes! All businesses should post pictures of their customers or employees if they are able to. Research has shown that posting pictures of people helps attract more likes and comments than if you didn't.

How Do I Write Captions that Do Not Annoy People?

Captions are one of the most tricky things about Instagram. You should limit the caption to about three readable lines because after you post more than 2200 characters, Instagram no longer shows your full caption. The best captions have about three hashtags and say something witty about the product. that way, people will remember.

Target Younger Audiences

This is especially helpful if you are a business that mainly serves young people. Most Instagram users are young adults around the ages of 18-30. You should remember this when you create your advertisements and decide if you want to invest so much on Instagram advertising or not.

Chapter 6: Come to Win! Cool Contests that Help You Make It Big Once You're All Set Up

If someone gave you a chocolate bar (or your favorite food) and said that you could have it if you just did one jumping jack, would you do it? Yeah, I bet you would. Let's face it, people like free stuff, even if they have to do something stupid to get it. Above that, people like to win. This is why having contests as a business account is such a necessity. According to a study by Tailwind, a company associated with Instagram, ninety-one percent of posts with over a thousand comments have to do with some sort of contest. These might be a little bit time consuming, but they are actually your best bet to marketing!

We discussed some of this in Chapter 2, but there are actually a variety of contests that can help your business grow even bigger. Contests help you interact with your customers. They help you advertise through your treasured customers. It keeps your own community engaged and also helps spread the word to people who may not have tried your product or service before. You do not even have to spend that much on the reward. Often times, even the smallest rewards will attract people. Your best bet is going with store credit because that means that the money comes back to you anyway (if you are a business that sells products).

1) Upload Your Own Photo Contests - This is the biggest gimmick that you can use to make your customers advertise for you. If you are a travel agency, you can

have people upload the wildest adventures that they have ever been on for a chance to win a $100 voucher to one of your tours. Hey, that also means that they have to spend whatever the difference is in your company - not your competitor's. If you are an Italian restaurant, you can have people upload the happiest memories they have eating pizza for a chance to win free pizza at your store for a month. Although you do lose some initial supplies and/or money, you will likely gain a long term customer. Not to mention, a lot of people will know about your business if you are just getting started out if there is a promotion going around.

2) "Like To Win!" Lotteries - This one depends on chance, but it gets a lot of people to like your post, which causes it to be shown a lot on their friends' "Explore" page. You can create a campaign to where people have to "like" your picture to enter a contest. Then, you get to draw a person out of a jar as a winner and offer them something. It's best if you give them a product that your company is selling, as this not only promotes your social media page but also your product as well.

3) "Fill In The Blank," Guessing, or Commenting Contests - You can see who knows more about your product or a company by hosting one of these contests. Perhaps you can reward those that answer the question right with a coupon code, or you could feature their profile on your business page. Either way, it is a fun little way to get the community engaged.

4) "Tag A Friend" Giveaways - This is the easiest way to get people who have not even heard of your brand to try a product. You simply tell someone to post a picture in your product or with your product (depending on if it is a food item, clothing item, or collector's merchandise). After they post it, they should tag a friend in the post

and then follow the store account. that automatically qualifies them to be entered in the contest, and you can select a winner through a random drawing.

5) In Store Picture or "Selfie" Contests - This works best if you actually have a storefront that sells products. Have people take pictures going to your store and then upload it online with a hashtag for their chance to win something. This not only entices the person to come to your store, but it also causes them to shamelessly advertise for your business on the internet. that will only help your business in the long run, even if you do give away a measly product. You can also feature your customers on your business page so that they know they are appreciated! The more a customer likes the management of a business, the more likely they are to come back, even if your product is not better than your competitor's.

Instagram contests take time to manage, and they can be a headache. However, it is the easiest way by far to reach everyone that you may want to connect with as a small business. Now that you know how to start a business account on Instagram and have everything set up, that is the best way you can continue to grow your customer base and increase in popularity as a product. Do not forget to associate each contest with a unique hashtag, or else you will be finding it difficult to keep track of everything on the post.

How Do You Host a Good Contest? Here Are Some Tips.

1. Make sure the rules are clear so that there is no dispute in who won or how to enter the contest! It is the worst thing that can happen if two people start arguing. It makes you look unorganized as a business, and you may have to give out two prizes instead if you cannot figure out who actually won.
2. Make a web page for the contest if it is big enough so people can make submissions there.
3. Don't make your contest last longer than a month! It can get tiring, and you might be too lazy to organize it by then. People may also forget about it, and the contest loses its purpose of getting your name out there.

The most important thing about any contest is that you need to keep it fun and interesting!

Now that you know how to manage these contests, you basically know everything you need to know to kick start your Instagram business today! If we could sum it all up, we would say that you need to separate your business account from your personal account to keep it professional. You need a distinct style for your brand and witty captions and posts that describe your product! Your information has to be correct, and don't forget to use hashtags and interact with your customers! Make sure you know who your audience is so that you can target them and others who are interested in the same stuff as them! Keep track of how you are doing through your Instagram Insights button, and create a location for yourself on the Instagram map! Once you do all of these things, you can start having live videos of everything that goes on in your business, answering all of your customers' important questions!

We hope that you have found this book useful. Even when you make it up there as a high earning business that attracts a lot of customers, these tips will still help you further advertise to even more people! Today's technology age makes it easy for you to advertise, and you might not even have to spend as much! Go get started on Instagram today; it is only one app download away.

Conclusion

Thank for finishing this book all the way to the end of *Instagram Marketing: A Picture Perfect Way to Strike It Rich!* We'd like to also thank Instagram for providing such a great social networking platform, so awesome that we were able to write a book about all the little marketing tricks that we can use through that app! We hope that we gave you enough information (and more) to make your business the next big hit on the Internet! Remember that our tips are not the only ways out there that you can use to show off your business to everyone else. Continue learning about online marketing, for it is for sure in the future of every businessman's life. You have the edge over your competitors now that you know all the tips in this book.

Now, get your nose out of this book! Your job now is to follow the steps in this book and apply it to your business now, or perhaps even start a new one and market through Instagram! Team up with other businesses and let your whole town (and people further than that) know that you have something great to offer! There is no reason to wait - the earlier you start this, the more people know about what you have to sell, and the more money will come your way!

If you feel overwhelmed or bogged down by all the stresses of your business already, consider delegating some work time to advertise on the Internet. Get this account set up during work hours by asking your employees to help you! If it can increase the number of people interested in your business, the one extra day of work will have been well worth it!

We wish you nothing but the best of luck in all your endeavors! We believe in you, and we know that you will make it big! If you succeed, that means we have succeeded as well in writing this book.

Finally, we would really appreciate it if you leave a review on Kindle! A lot of work was invested into this book so that you can take our tips and make it rich! Any comments are helpful for us, and we hope that this book was exactly what you needed to kick start your business online.

Check Out My Other Books

Below you'll find some of my other popular books that are popular on Amazon and Kindle as well. Simply click on the links below to check them out. Alternatively, you can visit my author page on Amazon to see other work done by me.

(www.amazon.com/Mark-Smith/e/B01JZ91Q5E/ref=ntt_dp_epwbk_0)

.

www.ingramcontent.com/pod-product-compliance
Lightning Source LLC
Chambersburg PA
CBHW071520210326
41597CB00018B/2823